HELLO, YOUNG ZOOLOGIST!

When I was a kid, I never thought I would get the chance to go to Antarctica. However, my love of animals unlocked the opportunity to head to the ice to study one of the coolest birds on the planet: the emperor penguin. Why do they have that yellow patch of feathers on their head? How deep can they dive? Get ready to find out! Emperor penguins are my favorite bird, and I hope they inspire you to explore the natural world.

Dr. Michelle LaRue

FACT FILE

SCIENTIFIC NAME
Aptenodytes forsteri

GROUP
Birds

FAMILY
Penguins

WEIGHT
85 lb (40 kg)

LIFESPAN
15–20 years

HABITAT
Sea ice

PREDATORS
Orcas and seals

CONSERVATION STATUS
Near threatened

WHERE IN THE WORLD?
Antarctica

SIZE
4 ft (1.2 m)

EATS

Krill

Fish

Squid

BEFORE YOU GET STARTED

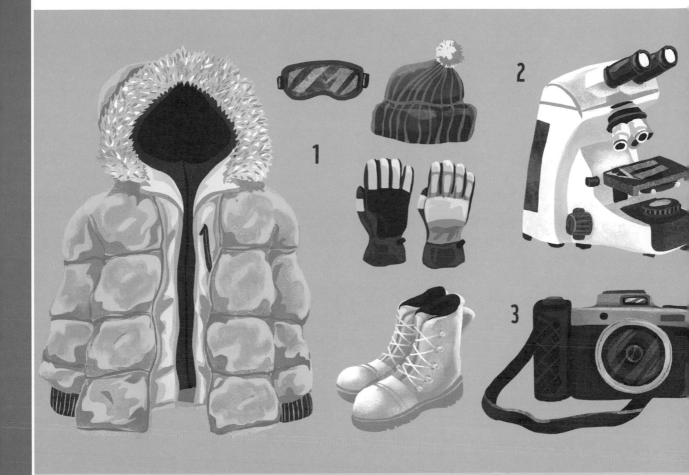

1 WARM CLOTHING

To work outside in Antarctica you need to be dressed in at least three layers. Pack long underwear, warm mittens, fleece pants, a cozy sweater, warm overalls, a goose-down parka, boots, a wool hat, and goggles.

2 MICROSCOPE

Sometimes scientists need to see things that are invisible to the naked eye to really understand penguins. Microscopes help us to see penguin feathers in fine detail, informing us about different diseases, or parasites that might be hitching a ride.

3 CAMERA

The easiest way to learn how many emperor penguins live in a certain place is to take pictures of them using a camera... and then count all of the birds you see in the photographs!

There are many things we can learn about emperor penguins. What do they eat? How many penguins are there? Where do they go in the winter? Scientists require different tools and pieces of equipment to get to the bottom of these questions.

Make sure you've packed enough food for your expedition!

4 HELICOPTER
Penguin colonies can be huge, so getting a view from the sky is essential if you want to know how many penguins live in a particular place. A helicopter can hover in one spot, allowing researchers to take lots of pictures. You'll need a pilot too!

5 FOOD AND DRINK
It's really important to eat a lot of food in Antarctica to give you energy and keep you warm. Field lunches might include sandwiches with freshly baked bread, fruit, cheese, and, of course, chocolate for dessert. Stay hydrated by drinking lots of water.

6 GPS TAG
GPS stands for "Global Positioning System." It uses satellites in space to track locations and movement. The tag is like a small cell phone that sticks to the penguins—it tells us every place they go.

MEET THE EMPEROR PENGUIN

Emperor penguins are marvels of nature. They are the deepest diving bird in the world, and they can survive the harsh Antarctic winters. It takes a tough bird to do that! Here are a few things that make emperor penguins so special.

STRONG MUSCLES

Some of an emperor penguin's strongest muscles are found in its breast. The penguin uses these muscles to swim.

BLACK AND WHITE

Having black backs and white bellies allows emperor penguins to blend in with the ocean when seen from above or below. This is a type of camouflage called countershading, which helps them hide from predators.

POWERFUL FLIPPERS

Emperor penguins can't fly. Instead they use their wings, called flippers, to power through the water at about 5 miles (8 km) per hour.

WEBBED FEET

These birds have webbed feet, like a duck. Claws allow them to grasp the slippery ice when they walk.

EYE SPY

Emperor penguins have a protective layer covering their eyes, called a nictitating membrane. It keeps the eyes from getting injured. Emperor penguins probably can't see the color red.

A group of yellow feathers next to each ear is called an auricular patch. Scientists think that this patch is used to attract mates and may signal to other birds how healthy an individual is.

Penguins have small, spiky-looking structures in their mouths that stop fish from escaping.

OPEN WIDE

The beak is a multi-functional tool for penguins. They use it to capture prey and to preen (clean) themselves. Their beaks are also useful for passing their delicate eggs between parents.

TAIL

Emperor penguins have small tails. Sometimes they use them to prop themselves up on the ice.

PENGUIN COLONIES

Emperor penguins live next to Antarctica's coastline on the sea ice. They rarely come onto land.

A CONTINENT OF PENGUINS

Antarctica is often thought of as the land of the penguins. But of the 18 species of penguins in the world, only two can be found exclusively in Antarctica: the Adélie penguin and the emperor penguin.

Did you know that there are probably more than 250,000 emperor penguins in the world?

A group of emperor penguins nesting together in the same place is called a colony. Emperor penguins form colonies in the winter time, when they need to stick together to survive in the freezing temperatures.

A TIGHT SQUEEZE

While most other types of penguins don't really like to be close to their neighbors, emperor penguins will huddle together for warmth.

LOOK FOR THE POOP

Emperor penguins are very messy, but it's not a bad thing! Scientists can see penguin poop (also called guano) from space using satellites. The brown stains show up easily on the white sea ice, revealing where colonies are located.

LIFE ON THE ICE

Emperor penguins make their homes on sea ice. However the places around Antarctica where they live can vary from one another, kind of like different neighborhoods. Here are some of the different landscapes where emperor penguins can be found.

PACK ICE

Pack ice is frozen water that floats in the middle of the ocean. Emperor penguins sometimes use it to rest after a long day of swimming—but they don't raise their chicks here.

FAST ICE

Frozen ocean water right next to Antarctica that gets stuck to the land is called fast ice. This specific type of ice is where we find emperor penguin colonies, and the penguins return to the same spots pretty much every year.

GLACIERS

Did you know emperor penguins are pretty good climbers? When the surrounding fast ice is too thin they will sometimes climb up onto frozen rivers called glaciers.

Emperor penguins need to stay warm, so a very popular spot to call home is in the shelter of a rocky outcrop, called a headland.

Of the 54 colonies of emperor penguins, only five colonies live near islands.

Sometimes the ice forms little nooks where the birds can hide to get out of the wind and cold.

PENGUIN EVOLUTION

If you stood in Antarctica 22 million years ago, it would look different, and so would the penguins that lived there! This is because groups of animals change, or evolve, over time.

EXTINCT PENGUINS

The emperor penguin is the largest penguin of all the penguins alive right now, but 37 million years ago there was an even bigger one! The biggest penguin ever discovered was the colossus penguin that lived in Antarctica. It stood nearly 7 ft (2 m) tall and probably weighed more than 200 lb (90 kg).

Colossus penguin

Spear-beaked penguin

Spear-beaked penguins that lived long ago probably speared their prey before eating it, rather than catching it in their beaks.

Being bigger can be an advantage—the colossus penguin could probably stay underwater for up to 40 minutes while hunting for prey.

ANCESTORS

A really long time ago, there was a type of bird that could both fly and dive into the water, kind of like cormorants can today. That is probably what the ancestors (like great-great-great grandparents) of penguins looked like.

Cormorants are seabirds that can fly. Penguins cannot fly, but they can swim, walk, and slide on their bellies.

Cormorants are happy on land...

Ancestors of emperor penguins probably evolved somewhere near New Zealand or Australia.

...and under the water!

THE FAMILY

Taxonomy is an area of science that focuses on classifying and describing life on Earth. It helps us learn how organisms are similar or different from one another. Penguins are grouped together in a family called Spheniscidae. Let's meet the others!

LITTLE BLUE PENGUIN

The smallest penguin in the world is called the little blue penguin, and it only lives in Australia and New Zealand. It weighs about the same as a bag of sugar and you could fit two inside a shopping bag!

AFRICAN PENGUIN

African penguins are the only species of penguin that live on the continent of Africa. They like to eat sardines and anchovies, and they look a lot like Magellanic penguins.

GENTOO PENGUIN

Gentoo penguins are the largest penguin in a group called the brush-tailed penguins, which includes chinstrap and Adélie penguins. Their tails look like brushes when fanned out.

CONTENTS

YOUNG ZOOLOGIST
EMPEROR PENGUIN

A FIRST FIELD GUIDE TO THE
FLIGHTLESS BIRD FROM ANTARCTICA

NEON  SQUID

WORLD OF PENGUINS

Penguins only live south of the equator, and most penguins do not live in Antarctica. In fact, New Zealand has the most types of penguins in the world!

Gentoo

Humboldt

African

Emperor

King

Magellanic

Little blue

Chinstrap

The red areas show where penguins live

Emperor penguins are more closely related to king penguins than to any other species.

Adélie

Galápagos

Royal

Macaroni

Snares Island

Southern rockhopper

Northern rockhopper

Fiordland

Erect-crested

Yellow-eyed

COPING WITH THE COLD

Life in Antarctica is filled with dangers, but one of the biggest threats is the cold. Ocean temperatures can get down to 28°F (-2°C), which is below the freezing point of water! Air temperatures drop to -58°F (-50°C) and the winds can be hurricane-like. Luckily, emperor penguins have a few tricks that help them keep warm.

IN THE HUDDLE

Emperor penguins huddle together to stay warm in the winter time. And everyone gets to take a turn being in the middle, where it's nice and warm—it can get to nearly 100°F (37.5°C)! Sticking together is the only way to survive.

WARM COAT

Emperor penguins have 12 different types of feather. Contour features help the penguins speed through the water easily, while other feathers called plumules keep the birds warm.

Emperor penguins also huddle
together to save energy.
They can go 100 days without
eating in the winter.

WARM FEET

Emperor penguins have a helpful system
that constantly pumps warm blood into
their feet to keep them from freezing.

LIFE CYCLE

Once emperor penguins are old enough to have chicks—about 6 years old—they start an annual breeding cycle. It begins with finding a mate and, if everything goes to plan, ends with a fat and happy chick at the end of the year!

1 MARCHING PENGUINS

In the late fall in Antarctica, during March and April, emperor penguins leave the ocean and travel over the ice to their colonies to find a partner. This is the beginning of their yearly life cycle.

2 MATING

Mating begins with courtship displays by each partner. This involves striking a pose and holding it for several minutes. It is thought to strengthen the bond between the pair.

3 INCUBATION

After being laid by the mom, just one egg is carefully transferred to the dad's feet. He will then incubate the egg (keep it warm) for up to two and a half months while the mom goes hunting for food out at sea.

5 SWAPPING OVER

When the mom returns, hopefully 7–10 days after the chick hatches, it's the dad's turn to forage in the ocean. They carefully swap the chick from the dad's feet to the mom's feet, and then the mom feeds the chick.

4 HATCHING

Hatching can take up to three days. When it is complete, the chick is fed a gooey substance called crop milk. This isn't actually milk. It's regurgitated food that is high in protein and fat.

6 FLEDGING

After several months of the mom and dad taking turns foraging, the chick begins to lose its soft, downy feathers. This is called fledging, and it signals that the chick is ready to swim for the first time!

21

A CHICK'S LIFE

HATCHING

In July of every year, emperor penguin chicks begin to hatch out of their shells. They're greeted with the frigid Antarctic temperatures—much colder than your freezer at home!

STAY CLOSE

As chicks grow, they need to stay off the ice because they could freeze to death. They do this by hanging out on their mom or dad's feet, snuggled in the warmth of their parents' belly flaps.

DINNERTIME

Emperor penguin chicks can't feed themselves, so they need to eat regurgitated food. That's another way of saying that their parents catch some fish, partly eat it... and then cough it back up and feed it to the chick! Delicious.

Life isn't easy being an emperor penguin chick. It's super cold and there's a lot to learn! The secret to success? Stick close to mom and dad for a while, and then things should be OK.

HANGING OUT WITH FRIENDS

Once chicks get big enough to walk around outside on their own, they begin to hang out with other chicks to stay warm. A group of emperor penguin chicks is called a crèche.

When emperor penguin chicks hatch they are about the size of a can of soup.

THE FOOD WEB

The Southern Ocean is home to lots of different life-forms (called organisms). They all play a role in the food web, which is a way of understanding who eats whom! Emperor penguins have an important role to play in the food web—both as predators and prey.

PHYTOPLANKTON

Phytoplankton are tiny organisms that are similar to ocean plants. They rely on the sun and a gas called carbon dioxide to create energy.

FISH

There are hundreds of kinds of fish in Antarctica. Most of them are endemic, which means they can't be found anywhere else on Earth.

GLACIAL SQUID

Glacial squid are related to octopuses. They are a favorite item on the dinner menu of emperor penguins.

EMPEROR PENGUINS

Emperor penguins eat mostly fish and crustaceans, which is a group of animals that include krill.

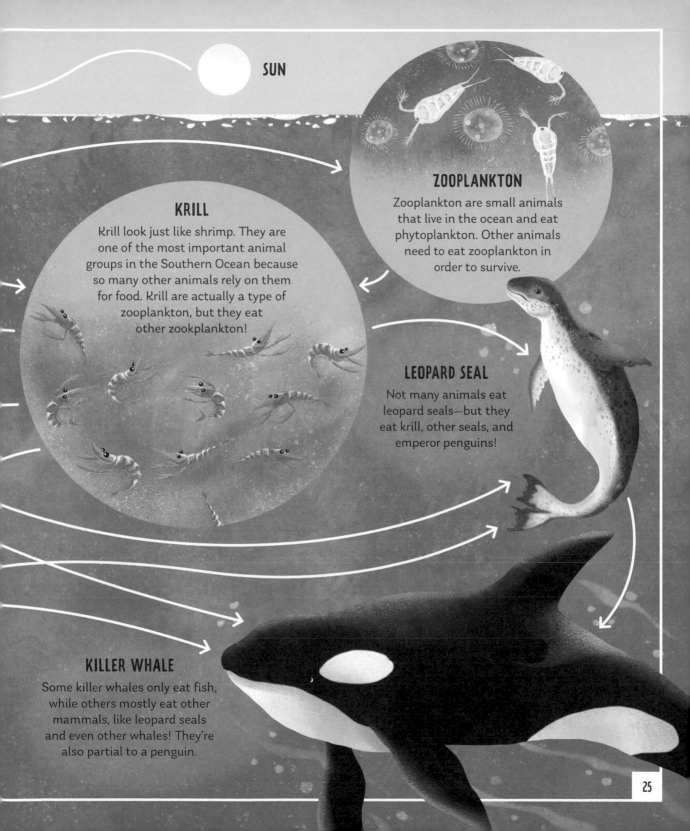

SUN

ZOOPLANKTON

Zooplankton are small animals that live in the ocean and eat phytoplankton. Other animals need to eat zooplankton in order to survive.

KRILL

Krill look just like shrimp. They are one of the most important animal groups in the Southern Ocean because so many other animals rely on them for food. Krill are actually a type of zooplankton, but they eat other zookplankton!

LEOPARD SEAL

Not many animals eat leopard seals—but they eat krill, other seals, and emperor penguins!

KILLER WHALE

Some killer whales only eat fish, while others mostly eat other mammals, like leopard seals and even other whales! They're also partial to a penguin.

DIVING DOWN

Emperor penguins can dive deeper than any other bird, and even farther than human divers. The reason they do this is to catch tasty fish and squid that live that live far below the ocean's surface.

Human
299 ft (91 m)

DEEP DIVERS

Emperor penguins comfortably dive deeper than other penguin species. They can't go as deep as a sperm whale, though!

Adélie penguin
787 ft (240 m)

Emperor penguins that are about to go foraging will stand at the edge of the ice before all jumping in together!

Turtle
951 ft (290 m)

Emperor penguin
1,854 ft (565 m)

Sperm whale
6,562 ft (2,000 m)

Emperor penguins like to dive during the daytime.

DIVING ADAPTATIONS

Over millions of years, emperor penguins got better and better at swimming and diving to catch prey way down in the dark waters of the Southern Ocean.

Emperor penguins are hydrodynamic—they are shaped like a torpedo, which means they can swim through the water easily.

Emperor penguins can hold their breath for a super long time. The record emperor penguin dive lasted 32 minutes, but most dives are less than 10 minutes.

When resting, emperor penguin hearts beat 75 times per minute. They can slow their hearts to 10 beats per minute at the deepest part of their dive.

Unlike flying birds, which have light bones filled with air pockets, emperor penguin bones are dense in order to help them swim.

CLIMATE CHANGE

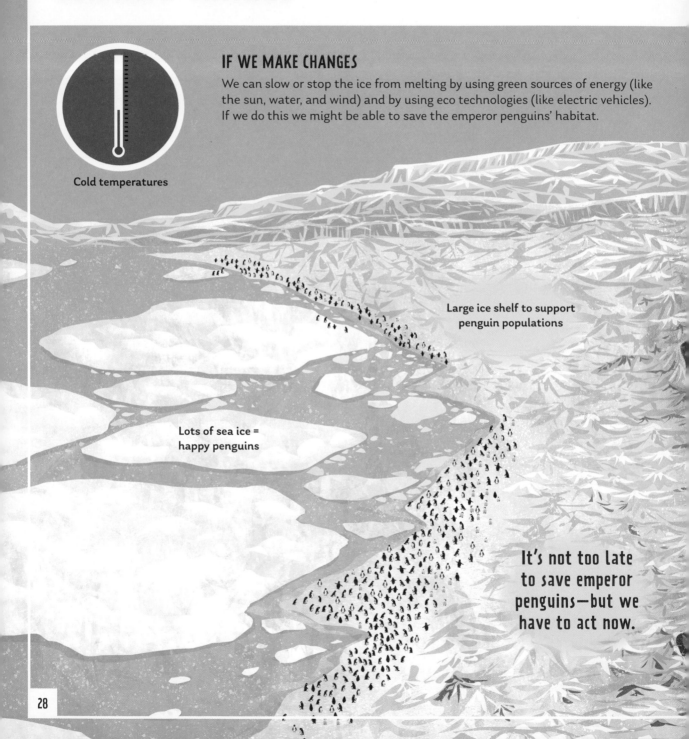

Cold temperatures

IF WE MAKE CHANGES

We can slow or stop the ice from melting by using green sources of energy (like the sun, water, and wind) and by using eco technologies (like electric vehicles). If we do this we might be able to save the emperor penguins' habitat.

Large ice shelf to support penguin populations

Lots of sea ice = happy penguins

It's not too late to save emperor penguins—but we have to act now.

Nowhere is safe from climate change. The more humans burn fossil fuels like oil and coal for energy, the warmer the sea and air temperatures in Antarctica will be, and the sea ice will melt. Emperor penguins are at risk—unless we make some changes.

IF WE DON'T MAKE CHANGES

If the gases from burning fossil fuels continue to increase, Antarctica could look pretty different in the future. For example, if there is less pack ice, it could be easier for fishing boats to get to places that were really hard to get to before. That could be bad news for penguins.

Warm temperatures

Small ice shelf

Rising sea levels

Increased fishing

Penguins won't want to live near human settlements.

TIME IS RUNNING OUT

Emperor penguins are very adaptable, but scientists don't know how well they can handle increasing temperatures or less ice. Predictions are that emperor penguins could be close to extinction by the year 2100.

Reduced sea ice = unhappy penguins

More grass would mean less space for penguin colonies.

GLOSSARY

Antarctica
The southernmost continent in the world. Antarctica is surrounded by the Southern Ocean.

Auricular patch
The patch of yellow feathers on an emperor penguin's head, right by its ears.

Breeding
When species mate to produce offspring—in the case of emperor penguins: chicks!

Camouflage
A way for an animal or plant to blend in with the environment around it.

Colony
A group of animals living together in the same place.

Crop milk
The first food that emperor penguin fathers feed their newly hatched chicks (but it's not actually milk!).

Evolution
Changes in the way species look or behave in order to better suit the environment they live in. These changes take place over a long time.

Extinct
When no more individuals of a species exist on Earth.

Fledging
When chicks lose their soft downy feathers and their adult feathers replace them.

Forage
To search for food.

Guano
Another word for poop!

Ice shelf
A sheet of ice floating on the ocean that is connected to land.

Incubation
The act of warming an egg so the chick inside can grow properly.

Parasite
A harmful organism that lives in or on an animal.

Predator
An animal that eats other animals to survive.

Preening
When a bird tidies its feathers by putting them back in place with its beak.

Prey
An animal that is hunted by a predator.

Sea ice
Frozen ocean water.

INDEX

This has been a

NEON  SQUID

production

*With all my love, Nic and Julian,
this book is for you.*

Author: Dr. Michelle LaRue
Illustrator: Pham Quang Phuc

US Editor: Allison Singer-Kushnir
Proofreader: Jane Simmonds

Copyright © 2022
St. Martin's Press
120 Broadway, New York,
NY 10271

Created for St. Martin's Press
by Neon Squid
The Stables, 4 Crinan Street,
London, N1 9XW

EU representative: Macmillan
Publishers Ireland Ltd,
1st Floor, The Liffey Trust Centre,
117–126 Sheriff Street Upper,
Dublin 1, D01 YC43

10 9 8 7 6 5 4 3 2 1

The right of Dr. Michelle LaRue
to be identified as the author of
this work has been asserted in
accordance with the Copyright,
Designs and Patents Act, 1988.

Library of Congress Cataloging-in-
Publication Data is available.

Printed and bound by Vivar
Printing in Malaysia.

ISBN: 978-1-684-49251-0

Published in September 2022.

www.neonsquidbooks.com